PET OWNER'S GUIDE TO THE
FERRET

Dennis Kelsey-Wood

RINGPRESS

PHOTOGRAPHY: KEITH ALLISON

ACKNOWLEDGEMENTS
Special thanks to Peter Pearson and the
Wakefield Ferret and Small Animal Rescue

Published by Ringpress Books,
Vincent Lane, Dorking, Surrey,
RH4 3YX, England

First published 1999
© Interpet Publishing. All rights reserved

ISBN 1 86054 135 6
Printed in Hong Kong through Printworks Int. Ltd.

CONTENTS

1

Introducing
The Ferret

Although the domestic ferret has existed in its present form for many centuries, the average person knows surprisingly little about it. Over the period of its domestication, it has become the subject of many half-truths and myths based on pure ignorance, rather than reality. Facts, legends and myths have become interwoven to create a pool of knowledge passed to successive generations. Consequently, the ferret, more often than not, has been treated very harshly, and, at the least, unfairly. In the following chapters, the true facts about this fascinating and delightful animal enable its real character and needs to be appreciated. Such information will help you to

The pet ferret is a domesticated polecat.

decide whether or not the ferret will make an ideal pet for your family circumstances. You will understand how to ensure your relationship with it develops on a mutually loving basis.

WHAT IS A FERRET?

The ferret is a flesh-eating mammal of the scientific group (an order) called Carnivora. This large group is subdivided into numerous other groups (families), which house many animals that share a believed common ancestral rootstock. One of these is called Mustelidae (the mustelids). It contains the ferret and all other animals loosely described as being of the 'weasel type'. These include weasels, martens, badgers, skunks, the wolverine, and other less well-known members. The weasels include species called by that name, but also those commonly known as minks and polecats.

The pet ferret is a domesticated polecat – generally thought to be the European polecat, whose scientific name is *Mustela putorius*. The domestic form has the name *furo* added to distinguish it from its wild ancestor. The word 'ferret' is derived from the Latin word '*furo*' or '*furon*' meaning a thief. Via old French it became furet

and thence 'fyrette' or 'firette' in Middle English. *Mustela* is Latin for weasel, while *putorius* is also Latin and derived from the word putor, meaning a bad smell. Later, we will discuss this matter of odour, and the reasons why it has become unjustly associated with these animals.

There are just three species of polecats: the European, already mentioned; the Turkestan (*Mustela eversmanni*), native to northern Asia and China, though it has now spread into Western Europe; and the Black-footed ferret (*Mustela nigripes*) of North America, where it is classified as an endangered species. The nearest relatives to the ferret, other than those already cited, are raccoons, coatimundis, pandas, bears, viverrids (civets, genets and mongooses), hyenas, dogs and cats – placed in the likely order of distance as relatives. Ferrets are not related to rats, mice, squirrels and their like. They are rodents – anatomically different to carnivores.

NATURAL HISTORY

Wild ferrets (polecats) are found in a wide variety of habitats, from lowland forests to meadows and semi-deserts. They may also take up residence in agricultural regions, living in outbuildings – even old houses – where they capitalise on the availability of an ample food source, usually small rodents. The Turkestan polecat is generally active by day, while its European relative is more crepuscular (active at dawn and dusk) or nocturnal. However, these animals are very able to adjust their periods of activity. This means that, if they are subject to human or other persecution, they will tend to become more active in periods that minimise this – night instead of day, or vice versa.

When sleeping, ferrets either dig their own den, or take over an unused rabbit, fox, or other ready bedroom. They may spend a great many hours sleeping, depending on how good the local food supply is. In places where this is hard to find, they must devote more time to travelling. Wild ferrets are loners by nature,

Wild ferrets live in a range of habitats ranging from lowland forest to semi-desert.

coming together in order to perpetuate the species.

Their main food items are small rodents and other mammals, such as rats, mice, hamsters, gerbils, voles, ground squirrels and rabbits. They will also take reptiles, lizards, amphibians, bird eggs, nestlings, and any ground or other birds that opportunity presents them with. Contrary to popular belief, they are not immune to snake bites, no more than is the mongoose. They simply become skilled at quickly attacking the snake, delivering a fatal bite to the neck before it can bite them.

Other food items include invertebrates (worms and insects), but fish are not part of the typical diet. Fruit and vegetables are only a very minor part of the menu; ferrets are unable to digest their tough cellulose walls. These items are obtained via the partially digested contents of their prey's stomach.

Enemies of ferrets are wolves, jackals, foxes, wild cats, feral dogs, large snakes and birds of prey. However, humans are their biggest enemy, either by direct persecution, or indirectly by destroying their natural habitats or prey species.

The ferret typically lives for six to eight years in captivity, and rather less in the wild state. However, domestic ferrets have been known to attain 15 years, so a well-cared-for pet could easily reach 10 to 12 years. A male is called a 'hob', a female a 'jill', and a youngster a 'kit'. A hobblet is a Vasectomised hob; a hobble is a castrated hob. With respect to size, the hob may attain 24 ins (62 cms) while the jill will be much smaller – as little as 14 ins (35 cms). Nearly half of the length comprises the tail. Weight is 1-5 lbs (0.45-2.3 kgs), the extremes being the summer weight for a small female and the winter weight for a large male. Both sexes display seasonal weight variation.

DOMESTIC HISTORY

It is generally thought that the ferret was first domesticated by the Egyptians – some say possibly before the cat. However, the evidence is debatable. Artefacts and paintings of certain animals, which include weasel-like species, are hardly accurate for identification purposes. It is possible that depictions credited as being ferrets are in fact the Ichneumon (*Herpestes ichneumon*),

The domestic ferret was developed for the sport of rabbit-hunting, and it is still used for this purpose today.

Aegean islands, where the 'polecats' remained to become an introduced species. Possibly the Romans, and certainly the Normans, took a semi-domesticated form of the polecat to Britain. There, as in most other European countries, it became a well-established domestic animal by the Middle Ages. It was transported to the Americas by early European explorers. In more recent times it was introduced into Australia and New Zealand to combat the rampant rabbit populations.

Although used as a general rodent controller, the domestic ferret was primarily developed for the sport of rabbit-hunting, dating back to Norman and earlier times. The many exits to a warren were covered with keep nets, and the ferret would be placed into an open burrow. This would panic the rabbits, which would bolt out of other exits to be caught as they made their escape. So that the ferret would not kill and eat the rabbits in the burrows, it would either wear a muzzle or a bell-collar to warn the rabbits of its presence.

All mustelids – and the ferret can be regarded as an archetypal example of the family – are

also commonly known as Pharaoh's rat or the Egyptian mongoose.

It is more likely that domestication did not begin until the Roman period – possibly about 300 BC. Certainly the Romans and Greeks used these animals to help reduce rabbit populations on some Balearic and tenacious predators. This is evident from an early age and shows itself in their constant desire to play and seek out things to do. This gave rise to the commonly used term 'to ferret out' – to industriously seek things.

PROS AND CONS

No pet species is all things to all people. This is certainly true of ferrets. In some ways, such as their playfulness throughout their lives, they compare with dogs. In others, such as their inquisitiveness and diet, they are more cat-like. Yet in other ways, especially as regards their management, it would be unwise to compare them with either of these pets. Take the ferret for what

it is and you will not be disappointed, or have unrealistic expectations.

REPUTATION

A feature of all mustelids is that, when alarmed or frightened, they eject from their anal glands a musky-smelling odour that their enemies do not like. The skunk is the most well-known mustelid to use this defence mechanism. More often than not, the ferret was handled roughly by ferreters. A consequence of this is that it would release its musky scent. Additionally, many ferreters used gloves to reduce the risk of being badly bitten. Ferrets were often carried around in sacks before and after working. Their housing was

A member of the mustelid family, the ferret ejects a musky-smelling odour from its anal glands when it is frightened or alarmed.

usually inadequate and unclean. Coupled with the ordeal of being muzzled, and the frustration this created when the ferret entered a burrow, the lot of the ferret left a great deal to be desired.

Not surprisingly, any opportunity to bite a human was taken. Thus the ferret's reputation for aggression and being smelly grew directly as a result of its terrible lifestyle. This has improved somewhat in more recent times, but, by then, the general reputation of this little mustelid was firmly established as being a rather unforgiving creature that could not be trusted and left a stench wherever it lived. Old notions and myths have a habit of staying around for a long while.

ODOURS

It would be misleading to say that ferrets do not smell, but let us put this into perspective. All animals have a natural body odour; there are no exceptions. Many also have scent glands, including cats and dogs, especially the males. These are used when the animal is in a fearful state, or when marking

territory, or both, depending on the species. Urine and faecal matter also create odour. A clear distinction needs to be made between these various odours, which can be removed or minimised by attention to their source, and combined general effect. They need be no problem at all if you are prepared to avoid them in the first place, just as you would with any other pet.

BITING

From an early age, ferrets love to play. Nipping and hanging on are instinctive to them, and would be essential in the wild. This is how they obtain their daily meals. In captivity, they must be taught the difference between humans and other pets they may play with. Handled and trained correctly, they will not display aggressive biting tendencies. If they do, it

When ferrets play they will nip and hang on to each other.

Obviously, nipping needs to be subdued when interacting with their human companions.

will be for one of the following reasons – they have been handled badly, and possibly infrequently; they have been allowed to get away with it as youngsters; they have an inherent aggressive nature due to poor breeding; or finally, they may have an injury or internal disorder that creates pain even when they are handled gently.

Ferrets are also individuals, so one pet may display a very different nature from another. Some are very gentle, others more robust in their play. Males are normally larger, so will be more powerful. This said, it does not mean females cannot be any more aggressive. Sex is not a criterion for belligerence.

VIRTUES MAY ALSO BE FAULTS

The virtues of these pets can at times be drawbacks – but this is true of most pets. For example, when you see a young kit scampering in an open drawer or cupboard this will highly amuse you. But when that mischievous juvenile hides something without your knowing, you may not appreciate this side of its personality. A playful nip from a youngster is rarely painful, but from an adult it will really hurt – this is no different to a dog, cat, or even a hamster.

DIET

With regard to feeding, ferrets are simplicity itself. The diet is

Lively and inquisitive, the ferret makes a fascinating pet for older children and responsible adults.

protein-based, the appetite very cosmopolitan. Special ferret foods are available for these pets, which can also be given good-quality cat diets and fresh meats. They will consume about the same as a small cat, so this part of their care is inexpensive.

OTHER PETS AND CHILDREN

There are no pets, unless they live in an aquarium, that can be regarded as ideal for children in an unsupervised situation. This is very applicable to ferrets. Generally, a child should be about eight or older before he or she can be considered suitable to safely handle these pets. Children have a tendency to be rough with animals. While a puppy or rabbit may tolerate this to a large extent, a ferret – or a cat – is less willing to do so. Cats will use their claws and teeth; ferrets will nip and may hang on. You should be aware of this and not blame the pet if it happens. Otherwise, do not obtain a ferret until children are older.

If other pets are already kept, common sense should prevail when deciding whether a ferret can be added to the family zoo. Obviously, you should never let a ferret loose with mice, hamsters, small birds, bunnies or guinea pigs. These are prey species to the ferret and will probably be killed, even though much of the ferret's killing ability is diluted in the domestic form. It will get excited and play-maul such small pets.

In reverse, be ever watchful of dogs and cats with young ferrets. These are natural predators themselves. They may badly maul, if not kill, the ferret in their excitement. When ferrets and dogs and cats are reared from a young age together, they invariably become very close companions. But always supervise playtimes in case the dog, in particular, gets over-zealous.

In concluding this introduction, it can be said that the ferret is cute, charming, playful, mischievous, and easy to keep – not at all like its reputation of old would suggest. On the down side, it needs lots of attention, is likely to play-bite more than some pets and, true to its type, will 'ferret' all over the place seeking things to carry around, corners to investigate, and places to sleep. It is certainly very different to most other pets you may have kept.

2 *Think Before You Buy*

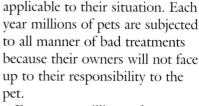

One of the sad things about many pet owners is that they do not think as much as they should before they purchase a pet. It is not enough to nod in agreement as this chapter is read, then ignore all the advice given in it. Potential owners should dwell carefully on the points raised, and genuinely ponder if they are applicable to their situation. Each year millions of pets are subjected to all manner of bad treatments because their owners will not face up to their responsibility to the pet.

Every year millions of pets, including ferrets, are abandoned or taken to animal shelters by owners who blame the pet for not being what they thought it would be. In 99 per cent of cases, the reality is that the owner is the problem. A very common excuse for getting rid of a pet is "I didn't know this or that fact." This merely indicates they never took the trouble to find out before they obtained the pet. And this problem is the tip of the iceberg. In many more cases, pets are not abandoned, but made to live a miserable existence under terrible conditions. It is hoped you will

When you take on a pet, you are responsible for all its needs for the duration of its life.

never be one of these uncaring pet owners who will add insult to injury by claiming they love animals!

WHY PEOPLE BUY FERRETS

The following are the most popular reasons people obtain ferrets, and my comments on these.

Cuteness: "It looked so cute and cuddly in the pet shop, we couldn't resist it." Ferrets are cute, but that does not mean you are capable of caring for them throughout their lives.

Novelty: "We wanted something different from the usual pets." That is fine, as long as you are able to cater for the needs of a 'different' pet. Be sure you understand what a ferret is all about, so you do not find 'different' unacceptable! Statistically, pet owners who purchase unusual pets, and ferrets are still within this category, do not have a good track record when it comes to keeping them for any length of time. In one poll, 70 per cent disposed of their ferret(s) at some time during its life. Similar statistics apply to other 'exotic' pets – pot-bellied pigs, hedgehogs, and the like. This does not mean the ferret is a bad pet – 30 per cent of owners keep them until the pet dies. It highlights the fact that casual pet owners rarely appreciate what is entailed in caring for unusual pets. These require dedicated, rather than casual, attention.

Pressure: "Our son/daughter pestered us for one, so we finally gave in." Never purchase any pet for a child unless you want that pet and are prepared to cater for all its needs if the child loses interest in it. If you are not that keen on ferrets, be firm and do not have one. Buy the child a toy, not a pet that will suffer when neglected.

Recommendation: "A friend has one – they are very pleased with it." This is a poor reason – you are not your friend and may not cope at all. Nor might they over a long period.

Freebie: "It was given to us for nothing." The initial cost of a pet is small when compared to its lifetime upkeep. If cheapness is a major criterion, forget about owning a ferret. You cannot afford one!

Pity: "We took pity on it – it looked so dejected." Never purchase a pet out of pity unless you are prepared to cope and pay out for any problems that may come with it.

Fashion: "We were told they are the 'in' pet." This is the worst reason to obtain any pet. What happens when another fashionable pet arrives on the scene? No animal should be obtained as a status symbol: sadly, many are.

Cash: "We were told we could make some extra cash breeding them." This is totally untrue.

Most breeders rarely break even with their endeavours – they subsidise their programmes.

WHY PEOPLE DISPOSE OF FERRETS

Odour: "They are too smelly." This is a sure sign the owner did not understand, nor effect, cleanliness in the pet's housing or general welfare. A ferret requires diligent attention to cleanliness. Ignore this and a home will slowly build up ferret odours. Do not blame the pet for your own shortcomings.

Count the cost before embarking on ferret ownership.

Aggression: "It is aggressive and bites people, including us, its owners." If the owner did not ensure that the ferret was easily handled when purchased they made their first, quite unnecessary, error. If it became progressively aggressive after purchase, the chances are strong they neglected it, or just did not handle it correctly.

Financial: "We could not afford the necessary regular vet checks and vaccinations, nor the bills when it was ill." The owners should have thought about these before the pet was purchased. Under normal circumstances veterinary bills will be very infrequent, other than for vaccination boosters which must be considered from the outset. Some allowance must also be made for illness costs. If cash flow is tight, it is best to forget a ferret until things are more fluid.

Time: "We really do not have the time to devote to the pet." It is most unlikely the average owner's circumstances could change so dramatically from when the ferret was purchased. What is really meant is that the owner has got bored with the pet, but does not want to appear as that type of person. If there is any possibility time could be a problem, admire, rather than own, a ferret. This displays honesty and the correct attitude.

Empty nest:: "Our children have outgrown the pet/left home." If you love your pets, you never outgrow them. If the child has left home this possibility existed when the ferret was obtained. Ponder this aspect carefully when purchasing for teenagers.

CRUCIAL CONSIDERATIONS

From the foregoing, and from years of involvement with a range of pets, and the people who own them, this author regards the following as the crucial considerations. You must be very honest in answering these.

COST

Can you afford one? The fact that you are convinced you would make an ideal owner is not enough.

It does not matter whether your inability to provide its needs stems from lack of interest or of funds – the result is exactly the same. In pondering costs allow for the following:

Have you got the time to spend handling and training your pet ferret?

- Purchasing a quality ferret from a reliable source.
- Buying the best housing for it you can afford in terms of both size and material construction.
- Ensuring you can afford to maintain its vaccination needs and future boosters, as well as periodic vet checks.
- Ensuring you can afford any reasonable vet bills that may come along from time to time.
- The cost of obtaining special ferret diets becoming a financial problem.

If you cannot meet all these needs it is best to wait until finances are better.

COMMITMENT

Do you truly understand the commitment needed? You must want to enjoy a high level of interaction with a ferret – and have the time to do so for its entire life. This is where most first-time, unsuccessful, owners fail.

Do you really understand what a ferret's features are? It has its own unique body odour. Only by experience of this – at a friend or breeder's home – can you really know if this would be acceptable. If you are thorough in cleaning, this is unlikely to be a problem. Ferrets may nip from time to time. If this would bother you,

Some countries have legal restrictions on owning ferrets.

forget a ferret – and a dog, cat, parrot, or any other pet that has teeth or a beak!

If you are positive about your ability to be a good owner, the chances are high that you will be delighted with these pets. It may be added that if you have a wide background of keeping various pets, your chances of being a good owner are better. You will already have experience of what true pet owning is all about.

LEGALITY

To conclude this discussion there is one more question you need to consider: the legality of ferret ownership. In most European countries there is no national problem, but there may be some local restrictions, depending on the area or town in which you live. There may also be restrictions if you live in rented property, or if you plan to breed with these animals. Check these with your local town hall and/or house owner.

In the USA, ferrets are illegal in Hawaii and Alaska. However, in most states, there are more regulations concerning ferrets than for dogs, cats, rabbits or other popular pets. This is especially so in California and other states that have only recently accepted ferrets as domestic pets. You must check with your local Fish and Game Department, as well as with county and local town halls. The fact that they are legal in your state does not mean they are legal in your residential district, such is the complexity of American state laws.

Potential American owners should also ponder a very sad but realistic fact of life. If a ferret bites someone and they report it to the Department of Agriculture (USDA), the pet will automatically be confiscated. It will be tested for rabies – which normally means it will be destroyed, even if it has been vaccinated against this disease. The risk of your contracting rabies from a ferret is infinitely less than from a dog, cat, or most other animals, including farm animals. But this fact, though known to most health officials, has not as yet been recognised within American legislation for ferrets and other pets still within the 'exotic and wild' category.

If you live in any other country there will be regulations of some sort – so check these before you proceed to obtain one of these pets, otherwise you might one day find your much-loved ferret being confiscated.

3 *Housing Your Ferret*

Historically, ferrets were normally kept outdoors. For the pet owner, 'in-home' housing is what is needed, and the only housing discussed in this book. This allows interaction between you and the pet at all times you are home. It enables the ferret to be familiar with household sights and sounds, so it is totally relaxed. This creates a more affectionate pet.

In the past, ferret hutches were made of wood. The main problems with these in a home situation are that they are almost impossible to keep clean and odour-free. Odour is able to penetrate even painted wood. Wood is also a much heavier material than wire of the thickness needed to make a strong cage. Aesthetically it is less pleasing, and affords less ventilation. In an outdoor location, wood is still the preferred material, but there the needs of insulation and protection from the weather become the main priority. Today, the use of chromium or epoxy-coated weld-wire cages are the best ways to house a pet. Such cages are easy to clean, amply ventilated, and available in a vast range of sizes, styles and furnishings. Prices will reflect their quality and features. Do not keep ferrets in aquariums. They are only suitable for small rodents.

THE FERRET CAGE

Once the decision to obtain a ferret has been made, the housing is your first priority. It should always be purchased ahead of the ferret. It avoids the problem of purchasing what was available at the time, rather than what was wanted, which can happen if pet and cage are purchased on the same day.

When inspecting a cage, ensure there are no sharp internal projections, and that the door size

A wooden hutch can be used for your ferret, but extra care will be needed to keep it clean and odour-free.

is ample for you to get your hand in and, with no difficulty, to get a ferret out. Those in which a complete side also opens are the best because they enable litter trays to be placed inside without difficulty. The larger the cage, the better. It should have room for an adult ferret to easily move around and exercise. Multi-level cages are more costly, but are better than single-level units. Your pet should not be spending too many hours in the cage – only overnight, or when you are not at home.

A solid floor is much better for the pet's feet than those of wire. In the wire cages, you can fit a rigid plastic floor. Commercially-made plastic floor rugs for cages may not last too long with ferrets, and might be harmful if pieces are swallowed. Line the floor with unprinted paper, towelling or similar material. Wood shavings are no longer recommended for small pets. It has been established that the phenols within these,

The bigger the cage, the better. Make sure it has solid-bottomed floor.

especially in pine, create respiratory and other problems on a progressive basis. They may shorten your pet's life, and reduce the efficiency of its immune system.

CAGE DIMENSIONS

The minimum cage size should be 62 x 62 x 45 cms (24 x 24 x 18 ins) but a larger unit would be better – as large as possible. The ideal indoor housing would be an indoor bird flight. This provides generous space to be furnished so one or more ferrets can really enjoy themselves when you are not with them. These can be fitted with castors for cleaning underneath or for relocating them. The distance between cage bars should be no more than 2.5 cms (1in), and half this would be better – especially for young kits. These pets can escape through surprisingly small holes. Be sure the housing is made of strong weld-wire.

CAGE FURNISHINGS

NESTBOX
A ferret needs a cosy place to sleep, so a commercial ferret nestbox is ideal. These are easy to keep clean. An alternative is a nestbox made for parrots, which can be disassembled. You can line it with rigid plastic for easy cleaning. The sleeping box need only be about 12 x 9 x 6 ins (31 x 23 x 15 cms) because these pets will curl in a ball when asleep. An entrance hole about 2.5 ins (6 cms) in diameter should be adequate for all but overweight pets. This box will give two ferrets a sleeping room because they tend to pile on top of each other.

There is a whole range of bedding options available for ferrets today. They include hammocks, tents and stylish bedrooms. The key considerations are that the pet has its privacy, and that the furnishings are easy to keep clean. Bedding for nestboxes can be towels, sheeting and the like. Keep a linen box for your pet so its bedding can be changed every day or two. Do not use wood shavings.

Place the litter tray as far away from food dishes as possible.

LITTER TRAY
This should be placed as far from the food dishes and nestbox as possible, though in a small cage this does not allow for much distance. Use a good-quality cat litter that will neutralise faecal and urine odours.

FOOD/WATER CONTAINERS
Inverted gravity-fed bottle-type dispensers are the most popular

A gravity-fed water bottle should be attached to the cage.

because ferrets tend to tip open-top water dishes over. However, an earthenware dog dish on the kitchen floor will be heavy enough to be ferret-proof, and will be a welcome change when the pet is roaming free. Food dishes clipped to the cage bars will prevent the ferret throwing the dish around, but crock-pots will also be fine, as are polished aluminium cat dishes. Avoid small plastic containers. If chewed, any swallowed pieces could create internal problems/blockages.

TOYS
Ferrets are so playful they will invent games with almost anything available. Some ideas are plastic sewer pipes they can run through, cardboard boxes with holes in them, towels, solid (never soft) rubber toys, and rope climbing ladders (ferrets are not expert climbers, but have fun trying!). They just love things like

hammocks they can relax and play in. There are many toys produced for these pets, but always inspect them carefully. Cheap toys may contain dangerous wire, or be of plastic, which the ferret can easily tear into pieces.

CAGE LOCATION
Pet housing must be located where the temperature is reasonably constant, never in direct sunlight or exposed to draughts – such as opposite

A number of toys are suitable for ferrets – check carefully to make sure they are completely safe.

external doors. Do not place it over or next to either radiators or air-conditioning units. Unless the housing is of indoor aviary type, it should be placed about two or three feet above floor level. This makes it easier for you to attend to chores, while giving the ferret a better view of what is happening in the room. Some owners have a ferret-proof room in their home, where the cage is located. However, it is better to have the cage in the room you spend most time in. Make that ferret-proof and everyone is happy.

FERRET-PROOFING

This term simply means making sure that any room in which the pet free-roams is carefully checked for dangers, and for places these agile animals might escape through or cannot easily be retrieved from.

The dangers are trailing electrical wires, cupboards containing potentially harmful contents (paints, chemicals, medicines), easily reached indoor plants (which might be poisonous), open fires, aquariums without hoods, power tools left running, irons left on a board or work surfaces with wires trailing to a socket (ferrets love to pull on things), open sewing baskets containing sharp needles, and anything else that an inquisitive ferret might want to pick up or explore.

It is also dangerous to leave

Ferrets are great escape artists, so you must ensure that you have 'proofed' all areas where they are allow to roam.

doors open when not protected from slamming due to draughts created by open windows, which themselves must not be open when the ferret is out of its cage. Kitchens are full of potential dangers: hot hobs, pans full of boiling liquids/foods, mixers and similar appliances.

Because ferrets are small and very quiet, it is wise not to let them roam freely in the kitchen while cooking and preparation are in progress; you could injure yourself and the pet if it was underfoot when you were carrying hot foods or plates. Be sure the ferret is not in the vicinity when any work involving power tools is in progress – or when you are painting – just in case your pet decides to involve itself, with dire consequences. The curiosity of a cat is nothing compared to that of a ferret!

Any holes in walls or skirting boards looking remotely large enough for a ferret to explore probably will be large enough, so must be sealed. Never leave washing machine doors open – especially if they contain clothes. To a ferret, this represents a great place to snuggle and have a nap, and the same goes for cupboards. You might close the door, and later be at a loss to find your pet. Food pantries must never be left open: a ferret will want to inspect everything, including items it will not actually eat. By nature ferrets are hoarders, so will transport all manner of unlikely items to places that seem ferret-logical.

By now it is hoped you get the general idea that a ferret really is a character unto itself. You must always be watchful for where it goes and what it can get up to. If it is possible to get into trouble, this is the champion pet of them all. It is one of their most endearing qualities, yet one of their infuriating traits – depending on the mood you are in! Regard a ferret as you would a little toddler.

THE OUTDOOR PEN

You cannot let a ferret roam freely in your garden or you will soon lose it. When outdoors it must be on a harness and lead. However, on a nice day, either place its cage in a shaded spot, or provide it with an outdoor pen. If the pen has a covered area, the pet will enjoy days in this, even if there are rain showers. An exercise pen is easily made using weld-wire of 1 x 0.5 ins (2.5 x 1.25 cms) hole size and with a gauge of minimum 19 (thickness of the wire). This is stapled on to a wooden frame to create panels of whatever size (length/height) are required. If the roof portion of the pen is hinged, this will make it easy to furnish the pen, but a separate access door within this roof is best for retrieving the ferret.

The pen may have a solid floor, or cross members if standing on concrete, or be of weld-wire if it will be placed on a lawn. At one end the roof can be covered to provide shade. The length can be whatever you wish, as can the height and width – the larger it is the more aesthetically pleasing you can make it, but the heavier it will be to move around. A permanent outdoor pen built on concrete, with side walls on which an aviary-type structure is positioned (though it does not need to be so high) can be furnished in a really attractive manner. You can feature rocks, logs, gravel, a shallow pool, climbing platforms and various herbaceous plants – a real garden enhancement. The extent to which you involve yourself with housing variations is limited only by your finances and imagination. The key factors with outdoor pens are that they must be very secure, with no gaps anywhere your pet could squeeze through. They must also provide shelter from direct sunlight and winds at all times. Ferrets love to bask in the sun, but must be able to retreat to a cooler spot whenever they wish.

Your ferret will benefit from having an outdoor run.

4 *Choosing A Ferret*

The first advice when choosing a ferret is never to rush this. If you do, you are taking the unnecessary risk of being disappointed within a very short time. Follow the advice given in this chapter. It will reduce the risk of purchasing the wrong ferret to a minimum. You will need to consider a range of factors, all discussed within this chapter.

Once you have determined your needs, make every effort to see as many ferrets as possible. Ask your pet shop, or vet, if they know of any local clubs. If so, go to one of their meetings. You will meet breeders, and arrange to see many of the colour patterns at their homes. A visit to a ferret show, if one is upcoming, is certainly the best way to see a lot of ferrets.

The best age to buy a ferret is between 10-12 weeks of age.

AGE TO PURCHASE

Ferrets are weaned at six to nine weeks of age. Any time after this they should be ready to go to new homes. It is prudent to obtain a kit of 10-12 weeks old. This gives the youngster time to overcome separation trauma from its mother, and that of moving to its first new home – if this is to a pet shop. Immediately after being weaned is a risky time. The immune system is not fully active, and the kit is in a high state of stress. Better to have a more established baby, able to cope with the moves at reduced risk of problems. The extra weeks make an enormous difference.

MALE OR FEMALE

Males are known as hobs, and females are known as jills. Neither gender makes a better pet than the other. Ferrets are all individuals; there are good and bad of both sexes. Males are larger, so this might sway you, but size is a relative state. There are small males and large females. You are advised not to let gender be an issue. Concentrate on getting the nicest ferret you can, regardless of its sex.

COLOURS

The way in which the colour pattern in ferrets is described is highly complex and dependent on which Association you belong to. Breeders do not always follow show standards, and may use their own terminology to add further confusion. The following is but a broad overview. There are six basic colours:

Albino: This is the all-white ferret

with pink eyes. It has no visual colour pigment at all. Genetically, it is not devoid of colour, but in its double gene dosage the albino mutation prevents pigments from forming. A very common colour.

Dark-eyed White: All-white with dark ruby eyes. Not an albino, but a separate mutation.
Black: Solid black from head to tail, with no pattern discernible.
Sable: Dark brown body, black feet, typical polecat mask. A very popular colour.
Chocolate: Like a sable, but the legs are brown and the body a slightly lighter colour.
Cinnamon: A dilute chocolate, reddish-brown, with legs of a somewhat darker shade.

MARKINGS
The colours are spread through a pattern, which embraces:
Mask: This is the way colour is imposed on the face in the form of a 'T' (full mask) or a 'V'. There may also be no mask.
Mitts: These are white feet (all four).
Blaze: This means white on the forehead and extending down the neck. It also means white on the bib (chest) and mitts on the feet.

PATTERNS
The main patterns are:
Siamese: Also called colour point. The body fur is lighter than that of the legs.
Roan: This is a mixture of coloured and white guard hairs.

Dalmatian: Spots and blotches on a white coat.
Silver: Dark grey (a mixture of dark and white hairs), some with mitts.

The colours and patterns may be intermixed to create an enormous array of possibilities, such as black roan, chocolate roan, Siamese cinnamon, Siamese mitt, or sable blaze. There are of course many ferrets with no show standard patterns, but are quite enchanting mongrels. A good ferret cannot be a bad colour – just like a horse!

Some colour patterns are more readily available than others, depending on the forte of the breeders in given areas. By seeing a number, you will soon decide which appeals most. Try not to be too specific. By so doing, there is the chance you may overlook a better-quality ferret because you are too picky over the colour. This said, if you really prefer one above all others, by all means stick to it – but be prepared to display patience in obtaining it and all other essential requirements, especially those related to health and temperament.

ONE OR TWO FERRETS?

Ferrets enjoy the company of their own kind and will form strong bonds with each other. Two will provide twice the amusement and companionship of one. When you are not around they will chase and play with each other just like kittens. For these reasons, two are recommended. However, upkeep costs will double. It is crucial you are able to afford the vet bills for two, otherwise you will end up not attending to booster shots and check-ups as regularly as you should. Do not negate this reality.

Ferrets are very playful and enjoy each other's company.

It is better to keep one as it should be kept than to keep two that are placed at health risk due to shortage of funds.

WHERE TO PURCHASE

Most ferrets today are purchased from pet shops. The second major source is from friends, or others who are disposing of their pet for one reason or another. Breeders are of course a traditional source. Animal shelters are also proving to be a growing source. It is not just adults that are available; there is usually an abundance of young kids during the breeding season.

This way they can be sure of getting a youngster, and one whose history is usually known. When you purchase a more mature ferret you really do not know what bad habits it may have developed, or the real reasons the owner wants to dispose of it. Few people will tell you the whole truth on such matters.

If you have aspirations to show your pet, the breeder is the best choice. They will have the quality and colour you wish to exhibit. However, if you just want a nice pet, your local pet store will probably be the most convenient source. They will be able to supply all your ferret needs. Never purchase from open market stalls, or animal auctions. These are fraught with problems. Any price savings may quickly prove to be very short-term.

It is very important that you select a reliable source. This is never easy to determine, but the conditions the pets are living under is a good start. These should be clean, never overcrowded, and never smelly. Food and water vessels should not be dirty or chipped, and the salesperson should be able to tell you all about ferrets. Avoid those who try the hard sell. A genuine seller will want to know if you will make a suitable owner. You might also ask your vet if they know anything negative about the establishment you decide to buy from. Ask other pet and ferret owners you may have met.

ASSESSING FERRETS

To avoid repetition, you are referred to the health chapter for details on the signs of ill health. Any ferret that looks unwell should not be purchased. A genuine seller will not have such a ferret on display. Never accept comments such as "he has probably got a minor chill and this will clear up in a day or so".

Take time to assess fitness and condition before making your choice.

Choose the ferret that is alert and inquisitive, and is used to being handled.

The pet you purchase should have received all of the necessary vaccinations, including any boosters. It should move around with no signs of a limp, and it should not appear lethargic once awake.

The matter of temperament is of paramount importance to your success with a ferret. If the seller shows the slightest reluctance in handling a kit, this will be because they are not sure whether it will bite them. Not a promising start! However, to be fair, an inexperienced assistant may be apprehensive if they are not familiar with those particular ferrets. Also, ferrets do differ in nature – some are a little bolder, and will try and play-nip, or nip if they are not in the mood to be handled. They are still in the learning stage.

However, any signs of obvious aggression indicate a ferret you should avoid. Once picked up by the seller, a young kit should relax very quickly and be handled with ease. Again, when it is passed to you it may show signs of hesitancy, but this should disappear once it is safely on your arm. This is the maximum limit of the problems you should experience.

Ideally, the pet will be a total darling and display no problems to anyone – this is the one I would want. It indicates that the animal was reared and handled correctly by its breeder before it was offered for sale. It removes any queries over temperament. Be aware that not all breeders are as attentive as they should be to this aspect of the stock they breed.

VACCINATIONS

Ferrets are no more immune to viral and bacterial diseases than any other animal. They must receive protection against these from a young age. Certain vaccinations can be regarded as obligatory. Others, together with conditions for which there are preventatives, rather than vaccinations, are more optional, though recommended depending on where you live.

CANINE DISTEMPER

Vaccination should be regarded as obligatory. Treatments are ineffective – the disease is fatal to ferrets. Whatever its source, a youngster should already have received one or more of its initial jabs. If it has not, find another

A programme of vaccinations is essential for the pet ferret.

supplier. The initial shot is given at six to eight weeks (earlier if the kit's mother's boosters are not current). Thereafter, two boosters are required at two to three-week intervals, then a booster each year.

FELINE DISTEMPER

It is generally thought ferrets are not susceptible to this disease. However, not all people agree, so it would be wise to protect against it. This is especially so if cats are in your household, or are prolific in your area, which they almost certainly will be. Your vet can give this shot combined with that for canine distemper.

RABIES

If you live in the USA, or other country that is not rabies-free, vaccination against this deadly disease should be regarded as obligatory. It may be legally compulsory anyway. It is given when the kit is 12-16 weeks of age, with a yearly booster thereafter.

HEARTWORM DISEASE

The ferret housed indoors is unlikely to be exposed to this mosquito-transmitted problem common in dogs. However, those living in the USA are at much higher risk than those in Britain. Diagnosis and treatment of these worms in ferrets is not without potential problems, so it is wise to avoid the condition in the first place if your vet recommends this. The drug Ivermectin can be administered orally once a month. It will destroy heartworms, and numerous other parasites as well.

FELINE LEUKAEMIA

Ferrets are rarely affected by this disease so vaccination is probably not necessary – discuss it with your vet.

WORMING

The seller should have routinely had faecal samples analysed for worms before the ferret was sold. However, if this was not done, you should do it at the earliest opportunity. An annual faecal test thereafter would be sound husbandry management.

SPAYING AND NEUTERING

All ferrets kept as pets (as opposed to those in a breeding programme) should be spayed (females) or neutered (males) when they are four to six months of age.

If spaying is not undertaken, the female's (jill's) life is placed at risk. Once she comes into oestrus (heat), she will not go out of this for about 150 or more days. During this time she may suffer bone marrow suppression. A consequence of this is likely to be acute anaemia and possibly death. Should she come into heat, this can be terminated by a hormonal injection administered some days, usually about ten, after the onset of the heat. She can then be spayed once out of oestrus.

In the male's case, neutering will dramatically reduce the odour created by hormones increasing his general body scent, which females find attractive. Desexing also makes him more placid and unconcerned about satisfying his sexual drives.

DESCENTING

Although many pet owners have their pet's scent (anal or musk) glands removed, this is unnecessary. It is generally not advised unless there are sound medical reasons for this. The scent glands are only used when the ferret is frightened, or in a highly excitable state. It will not normally be in these states as a pet, so descenting will have no effect on body odour. Further, should the pet by chance escape from its home, and be confronted by an aggressive dog, cat or whatever, removal of its scent glands will have denuded it of a vital defence mechanism.

ACCESSORIES

Additional to the items discussed in the housing chapter, there are other accessories recommended from the outset. A medium soft bristle brush, comb and soft cloth will be useful for grooming and polishing the fur. A pet carrier is a definite must for transporting your ferret to the vet or elsewhere. Any that are suitable for cats or rabbits will be fine. The rigid fibreglass types are better than those in plastic or cloth, as general utility boxes.

A first aid kit is certainly worth having; its contents are discussed in the health chapter. A small harness is useful so the pet can become familiar with wearing this. Be sure it is suitable for ferrets. It must be a comfortable

You will need a carrier to transport your ferret to the vet.

The price you pay will depend on age, quality, colour, and whether it has been vaccinated.

fit, but secure so that the ferret cannot wriggle out. It should be used only when the pet is being exercised, or when visiting the vet or your friends. Collars are not recommended.

COST

The cost of a ferret is dependent on numerous factors. These include its age, vaccination status etc., colour and quality. However, a typical ferret from a pet shop, or reliable breeder, will cost rather less than a purebred puppy or kitten. You are advised to obtain prices from various pet shops and breeders. This will establish what the current market prices are. Always be prepared to pay the extra cost of a kit that displays a charming and inquisitive personality.

5 Care and Training

When the exciting day arrives to collect your new family member, try to do this in the morning. This allows the ferret to settle into its new home during the day. You will be around to keep your eye on this process. Be sure you take your pet's carrying box with you, or at least a stiff and well-ventilated cardboard box lined with old towels.

Make the return trip home as quick as possible. Do not stop at friends' homes to show off your pet and, if the journey is long, do have short breaks. The ferret must not be exposed to draughts in the car, nor must it ever be left unattended in it during hot weather. Many pets die every year due to lack of ventilation in unattended vehicles – heatstroke is fatal to pets.

Give your ferret a chance to settle when he first arrives home.

PAPERWORK

Be sure you are given your pet's paperwork. This will include vaccination certificates, pedigree (if applicable), receipt, diet sheet, and details of any preventative treatments (e.g. worming) recently effected. A current health certificate is usually available, but you may have to pay its cost. It is certainly useful if the pet comes with a limited time guarantee. Obtain a supply of the pet's current diet items. These should be maintained during the first stressful days of the ferret's home move.

ARRIVING HOME

Once home, place the ferret into its housing and allow it to explore; it may wish to have a snack and a snooze. Let it settle in for a few hours, and do not let the children pester it during this period. Later, it can be allowed out so it can explore the room, and play a little. Initially, its freedom should be restricted to one room. Be sure this contains a litter tray. Do not let the pet into other rooms until you are satisfied it knows what a litter tray is for. Then place trays in each room it has free access to.

The ferret will usually use the toilet shortly after waking up, after playing, and after meals. At these times you can place it periodically into its tray until it gets the general idea. Remember, if you allow free access to roam through numerous rooms before your ferret is trained, you may start to have problems, so start correctly.

HANDLING

It is most important that your pet is handled gently, but firmly. If not, this will increase the possibility of it nipping. This fact must be impressed on young children, and strictly enforced if you want the best from your new family member. Always be sure the pet is aware it is about to be handled – it should be able to see you. No sudden lifts when it is asleep, only half awake, or not watching.

There are two ways a ferret can be lifted. The most usual is to firstly place one hand over its shoulders, the fingers encircling its chest. This restricts its movements. It can now be lifted, at the same time having its rear end supported with the free hand, which is passed under the first hand so the body will rest on your arm. The second hold is by

HANDLING

1. Take a firm hold, with one hand encircling the chest, and the other restraining the hindlegs.

2. As you feel the ferret begin to relax, the hold on the hindlegs can be lighter.

3. Now the ferret is being held with just a light hand on the tail.

4. The ferret is completely relaxed, and makes no attempt to escape.

grasping the loose fur at the base of the neck and lifting. The pet will relax because this method mimics the way it was carried by its mother as a baby. You can then support its rear end with your free hand, which is more comfortable for the ferret. With regards to disciplining a ferret that nips your hand, the answer is a stern "no" accompanied by a light tap on the snout. Never attempt to make any discipline harder than this – it will prove counter-productive.

GROOMING AND BATHING

Regular grooming is extremely important; it stimulates healthy skin and fur. It removes debris from the coat and is a great means of interacting with the pet. Always start by briskly brushing the coat with its lie, then gently comb likewise. Do not apply too much pressure, especially on sensitive parts (the belly and tail), but enough to be thorough. Nails should be checked; if they are too long, using manicure clippers, trim the ends. Be sure you do not cut close to the quick (the pink area) – this is a blood vessel. It will cause pain, the nail will bleed, and the ferret will not be very keen on your doing this again!

Inspect the ears to see they have no smell or signs of wax. Using a cotton bud you can gently wipe wax away using tepid water. Never probe too far into the ear. The teeth should be inspected for any signs of problems – incorrect alignment, damage, or tartar. Your vet will periodically clean the teeth for you to prevent tartar build-up.

Contrary to what might be thought, bathing does not reduce the body odours of ferrets. It removes much of the natural skin oils in which the odours are contained. However, to compensate for this loss, the body increases the production of oils. The pet is soon back to its normal state. Bathing will remove surface dirt and ingrained non-body odours. Every six weeks will be often enough, and with regular grooming, your ferret can go for months without a bath. Use a special ferret shampoo, or one for cats.

ODOUR CONTROL

The ferret's reputation for being odorous has been greatly exaggerated over the years. Its normal body scent is different to that of other pets. Many owners find it not unpleasant. The key to ensuring it remains that way is scrupulous attention to

1. Ferrets need regular grooming.

3. Nails may need trimming

2. Comb with the lay of the coat.

cleanliness. This avoids the situation where odour piles on odour, which is why any pet can appear to leave an unwanted smell.

In particular, attention must be paid to the ferret's litter tray and bedding. The tray must be cleaned at least once per day, more often according to usage. Bedding should also be renewed each day, or at the least every few days, and the pet regularly groomed. Carpets should be vacuumed daily, and food dishes washed.

Should you find the pet has fouled any area of the floor, this

BATHING

1. The domestic ferret should be bathed every six weeks.

2. There are a number of shampoos specially designed for ferrets.

3. Make sure all the shampoo is rinsed out before towelling dry.

4. The ferret is surprisingly easy to handle in this situation.

should be washed and an odour-neutralising chemical, from your pet shop, placed on it. Scented aerosols are useless for removing odours, they merely mask them for short periods. It is useful to cover the spot so the pet cannot reuse it. If a certain room is often fouled, do not allow your ferret access to it, and make sure it is thoroughly cleaned.

Be sure there is no trace of scent before the ferret is allowed access to that room again. Odour molecules can penetrate furniture, taking some time to disappear. If by chance the ferret should have occasion to use its scent glands, do not worry. The smell is temporary and soon dissipates into the air. It does not linger like that of a skunk.

HARNESS TRAINING

Ferrets may be compared to cats where training is concerned. For example, they cannot be taught to heel like a dog, but will want to go their own way when on the end of a harness and lead. At best, you can arrive at a compromise whereby they are allowed to sniff around to satisfy their curiosity, but will make progress with you once they feel a few pulls on the lead.

When lead training, you must start by letting the ferret become familiar with the feel of its harness (never a collar) while in your home. Be sure the harness is a comfortable, snug fit, but be warned – few harnesses are 100 per cent escape-proof if a ferret really becomes alarmed! Your supplier will find the one that fits just right – do not buy it if it does not.

Training is a case of walking the ferret in your home with the lead attached. Initially, let it go where it wants. Slowly introduce restriction on its movement and encourage it to follow you by calling its name. It may take some days, but eventually it will understand and show some willingness to comply. But remember, it is a ferret; if you want a dog, buy a puppy!

REWARDS

The ferret can be taught to do a number of things, but always on the basis of persuasion and words of praise – never admonishment. A tidbit is always a useful training aid when teaching your ferret simple things like standing on its hind legs or jumping.

Always bear in mind that the best way to train any animal is to

HARNESS TRAINING

1. With careful handling, your ferret will accept the harness and lead.

2. The harness is fitted over head.

3. It is then fastened behind the front legs.

4. The next step is to attach the lead.

5. In time, the ferret will enjoy lead-walking as a regular exercise routine.

focus on the things that come naturally to it.

For example, it will be easier to teach a ferret to run through a series of tubes for a reward than it will to teach it to sit like a dog. Place the ferret at the end of the tube while holding a tidbit at the other end. It will soon scurry through for it. Add another tube, and before long it will run through many with twists and turns just by being placed at one end. Next, give the tidbit only every second time, and the ferret will still oblige.

Eventually, just the occasional treat will be sufficient – the rest of the time lots of fuss will be adequate reward.

WORKING FERRETS

The tradition of working ferrets goes back to Norman times, and the sport of rabbit-hunting remains popular to this day.

Ferrets are transported to the site in specially made boxes, and they are confined while a thorough reconnaissance of the site is made. Purse nets are set over all the exits, and these must be skilfully placed in order to capture the bolting rabbits.

It is now time for the ferrets to start work. Nowadays, the ferret is usually fitted with an electronic detector, and this makes it easy to keep track of what is going on underground.

Once released into the burrow, the ferret will travel through the tunnels, causing the rabbits to bolt. The ferret may make a kill underground. If the ferret fails to find any rabbits, it may return to the surface, and in this case, it should be put down another burrow.

When all the rabbits have vacated the burrow, the ferret needs to be recalled. This is often done using a recognised call or sound. This sound is always used at feeding times, so the ferret learns to respond to it.

WORKING FERRETS

1. A reconnaissance of the area is needed to find all the burrows.

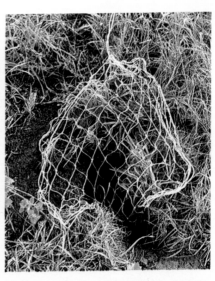

2. It takes skill and experience to set the purse nets over all the exits.

3. The ferrets are transported to the site in a specially made box.

4. An electronic detector is fitted to the ferret.

5. Once released, the ferret will start working its way along the tunnels.

6. The bolting rabbit is captured by the net.

When all the rabbits have left the burrow, the ferret will emerge, usually in response to a recognised call.

6 Feeding Ferrets

The content of the ferret's diet today has changed dramatically from that which persisted a decade or so ago. For one thing, specially formulated commercial diets that existed years ago only for research institutions and zoos are now commonplace for pets. The moment the ferret started to become a fashionable pet, food companies started to study and develop 'complete' diets that appealed to the pet and, via attractive packaging, to owners.

You can feed your pet a diet that is very convenient, and has a

A good-quality, balanced diet is the key to a ferret's health and wellbeing.

good shelf life. Alternatively, you can take a more traditional view of the subject. You can prepare meals, as in the past, from fresh foods, or you can combine old and new approaches to feed a blend of the two types. This author has always taken the latter path, on the grounds that it enables the pet to gain from the benefits each has to offer. Let us examine the pros and cons. You can adopt the one you feel is more suited to your particular situation or views.

COMMERCIAL DIETS

These are available in semi-moist, moist, or dried form. They are prepared under high standards of hygiene, and are blended to include all the known dietary needs of these carnivores. No other foods need be supplied, other than water, and maybe a few treats. Some have impressive track records, developed after extensive studies and use in zoos and laboratories. Others have less impressive credentials, having been rapidly developed to take advantage of the explosive growth in the market (there are estimated to be six to ten million pet ferrets in the USA alone).

Bear in mind that moist diets provide virtually no jaw exercise for the pet, nor do they help clean the teeth. A major consequence of this in dogs and cats is reflected in the steady increase in dental problems. The same scenario is almost certain to happen in ferrets. The dry diets are better in both respects. They also remain fresher once their packaging has been opened, and have less appeal to flies and other insects. Formulated diets are fortified with vitamins after the cooking process to ensure no loss of these from the heating process.

On the down side, 'complete' diets do not provide the same level of appeal. They do not allow the pet to have any choice of dietary items, which I have always felt is as important to pets as to humans. Commercial diets may satisfy the metabolic needs of animals, but not their total psychological needs. This aspect of food is often ignored in the quest to provide convenient foods, with long shelf lives, and which can be appealingly packaged to appeal to the owner.

TRADITIONAL DIETS

Through the centuries, until recent times, ferrets were fed diets which ranged from those that,

Until recent times, ferrets were fed on rabbit carcasses, day-old chicks, and other meats available at low cost.

even by today's high standards, were nutritionally excellent, to those which just about kept the ferret alive. If we consider only the good diets, these were comprised of whole rabbit carcasses, day-old chicks, fish, tripe, paunch and other meats available locally at low cost. Some vegetable matter in the form of mashes was given, along with small quantities of milk, honey, and water.

The ferret ate the lot, including

the fur, feathers, and bones. It would be untrue for modern dieticians to say these regimens were inadequate. The ferrets were extremely fit, hardy, virile, and rarely suffered from dental and other now common problems, such as obesity. The ferrets were worked on a regular basis and were, to quote a phrase, 'tough as old boots'.

However, these ferrets were not indoor pets, and owners devoted more time to preparing the meals than the average owner of today wants to. Because the ferrets were given whole or part-carcass items, they gained the necessary vitamins from the liver and other organs, as well as from the stomachs of the food items, much as a wild polecat will. The very natural form and range of foods in their diets was sufficient to ensure they received vitamins and minerals, as well as proteins, fats and carbohydrates, in a reasonably balanced ratio and amount.

On the down side, the very natural form of the foods also meant they might have contained fleas, lice and other interesting wildlife! Disease vectors were readily transported from the food to the ferret. The problem with these old diets is not that they were inadequate, but that they were time-consuming to prepare, and carried a high risk of potential health hazards that the modern owner simply cannot afford to take. The young death rate was much higher than today, which was true for most domestic animals.

Today's pet owners can obtain high-quality meat and poultry that carries no health risk. But, because they are not expert on the nutritional needs of a ferret from the composition standpoint, they must ensure that compensation is made for things like fur, and vitamins and minerals not present in choice cuts of beef or chicken. If traditional foods are the main dietary items, it becomes essential to have a sound knowledge of the constituents of food items supplied. Commercial diets take all the guesswork out of feeding regimens.

SUGGESTED DIET

To ensure your pet lacks no important dietary ingredient, the staple part of its diet should be a commercial ferret or cat brand. Dog diets contain more carbohydrates than those for cats. Ferrets are more akin to cats in protein needs (about 32 per cent),

The modern option is to feed a complete diet which caters for all nutritional needs.

so do not feed formulated dog foods. Even with cat foods, choose the better brands. Ferrets are not natural fish eaters, so give these sparingly. Try a few brands of popular ferret/cat foods, both dry and moist, so you can see which your pet likes best.

In order to provide interest and dietary stimulation, you can replace a day's commercial menu with one of fresh meat or poultry. Meat can be given raw or cooked – as long as it is fresh butcher's meat, and not from a source unfit for human consumption. A ferret will appreciate beef and similar bones. They are good for jaws and teeth. When feeding meats, cut them into small slices the pet can cope with. Avoid chicken, rabbit and fish that contain bones; these are small, or may splinter when bitten, and get lodged in the pet's throat or digestive tract.

You can give a ferret a small

sampling of fruits and vegetables to see which have appeal. Do not worry if little is eaten. Ferrets are not herbivorous, so such items are not important to their diet, only according to individual tastes. Milk is unnecessary – and too much will create internal disorders. Never feed chocolates, sweets, biscuits, cakes and similar. These provide no benefit, yet can cause loss of appetite for the main dietary items.

The occasional hard dog biscuit will not be dangerous, and will help to keep teeth clean and give the ferret something to play with.

Dietary supplements – vitamins or minerals – should not be routinely given. If the diet is well balanced, an excess of these can cause hypervitaminosis. More is not always better! Supplements and tonics should only be given if needed. Any query on this should be discussed with your vet.

WHEN TO FEED

Ferrets have a rapid metabolism; little and often is the ideal way to feed them. However, they are adaptable to your timetable, and the use of dry ferret or cat foods can be used to meet both of your

Vitamin and mineral supplements are available, but consult your vet before supplementing a complete diet.

needs. The main meal can be given in the evening, with an amount of dry foods left in a separate dish to be eaten as wanted. If you can provide two small meals a day, this is better than one large one. If your pet starts to become obese, reduce the amount of dry foods given on a free-choice basis.

A key point with feeding is that main meals are given at about the same time each day. The pet's digestive system runs like a clock, and the ferret will look forward to seeing what is on offer. Its bowel movements are regulated by the feeding times so, for numerous reasons, keep to a schedule.

HOW MUCH TO FEED
This is dependent on many factors – age, exercise level, breeding state, time of year (temperature), quality of the diet, and the individual's metabolic efficiency.

Ferrets prefer to be fed two small meals a day.

Stating fixed amounts can be very misleading. As a very general guide, a typical pet will consume 3-4.5 ozs of quality meat per day. A better way to establish requirements is to divide the quoted amount by the number of meals – say two. Place the food in a dish and see how much the ferret eats within 15 minutes. If the amount is quickly devoured, add more until the pet loses interest. If some is left, note the amount. Repeat at the next meal. By this process you will, within a day or two, establish how much you pet needs, and can adjust up or down accordingly. The total weight of food should include dry food. A pet will consume more of a low-quality food than of a high one. Bear this in mind if you are thinking that cheap brands will save money – not quite true if the pet is to be fed its nutritional needs.

Feeding any animal is not an exact science. It is a mixture of common sense, dietary knowledge, and knowing each pet very intimately. Feeding should never be reduced to a mundane chore, but made as interesting for the pet as you want your diet to be. Finally, when adding unfamiliar items, never do this in glut form. This is sure to create problems. Always add in small quantities on an increasing daily basis. This allows the digestive flora adjustment time to cope with them.

OBESITY

Pets become overweight for the following reasons: they are not getting enough exercise in relation to food eaten; they are eating out of boredom – it has become a habit to try to overcome boredom; they are being fed an incorrect diet – too much carbohydrate or fats; or they may have a metabolic disorder that the vet can advise on or treat.

With ferrets, another reason must be added. During the autumn months these animals invariably gain weight. This is a quite natural process. In the wild, this extra fat layer would provide insulation and food reserves. It could happen with pets, but, given their regular dietary habits, will not be as pronounced as with their wild cousins.

7 Breeding Ferrets

The first-time owner is strongly advised not to consider breeding ferrets. Rather, keep one or two until you know what is entailed in their management. By that time your pets will have been neutered. Any thoughts of breeding would require stock bought specifically for this purpose. Unlike the situation with other animals, you cannot realistically commence casual breeding with ferrets to have the occasional litter because of the need to neuter at an early age.

Unless you are very dedicated, there is no point in breeding these pets. Even then, you must have very fixed objectives in mind. They entail a lot of hard work, and the potential returns will not cover your investment. There is no shortage of ferrets, so every additional small breeder helps to suppress the existing moderate prices.

Each year, as with all other pets, enthusiastic beginners commence breeding only to find the truth of what is said here. They quickly get in over their heads and rapidly lose their initial enthusiasm. Disappointed, they leave the hobby within a couple of years of entering it. Do not become part of this scenario.

In this chapter we will look at numerous considerations you should bear in mind, and prepare for, if the idea of breeding presently appeals. By the time you have gained practical management experience you will be ready to start a small breeding programme with a greater chance of it being successful.

Alternatively, you will realise just what is involved and may decide that breeding is not for you after all. You will be glad the advice here was heeded.

Practical breeding cannot fairly be covered within a book written for in-home pet keepers.

Breeding ferrets should not be taken on by the first-time owner.

Therefore, at the end of this discussion, only the basic breeding facts related to these animals is given; they will serve as a reference platform for you to build on.

BREEDING OBJECTIVES

Any breeding programme must have a definite objective. To breed for its own sake, meaning just to produce offspring, is pointless, yet many pet owners do just this.

Here are the three prime targets for hobbyists.

To specialise in the less-established colour patterns:
The advantages of this is, if demand for these increases, you will be ideally situated to capitalise on it. You will become a breeder associated with the colour pattern. Prices for the unusual are always higher than for those readily available, sometimes ridiculously so for short periods. The gamble is that, if the colour pattern does not gain popularity, you may find it difficult to sell the youngsters. You may have to search around to find initial stock, and it may be more costly if the market is currently rising for it. You are advised to attend shows and find out what the situation is with the colour pattern, and become an exhibitor once you get underway. This helps to promote you and the colour pattern.

To specialise in quality show stock: In this instance you choose any colour pattern, usually one that is well established. You then attempt to improve the standard of conformation and colour pattern in each successive generation. You must become a

successful exhibitor yourself to achieve your objective. But, ultimately, the value of your stock will increase. This is the most popular definable objective within the hobby, but it is fraught with problems.

You must commence with excellent (and thus more costly) stock, and competition is fierce – many others are trying to achieve the same objective. But breeders enjoy this side of the hobby. It enables them to meet many other hobbyists, but can be very time-

consuming – something that must be carefully considered. It usually takes quite a while before you become well established.

To specialise in quality pet ferrets: With this, you will be especially concerned with temperament, which does not mean that conformation and colour pattern are unimportant. They are; you need to stock the colour patterns that will sell in the greatest numbers. Your initial stock needs to be generally sound,

but outstanding in its temperament. With every generation, this aspect becomes the prime consideration.

Your market will be direct sales to pet owners and shops. While this may seem an easy target, it has its problems. Pet shops need stock they can resell at a profit, so your pricing must be competitive. You will probably need to breed more ferrets than for the other objectives, and be very efficient at management. There are numerous commercial companies who breed on a large scale for this market. Nonetheless, with hard work, you can build up a steady repeat business to pet shops – the direct sales represent the icing on the cake.

YOUR STUDY NEEDS

For any worthwhile breeding programme you will need to have a wide knowledge of many subjects. These include nutrition, record keeping, general husbandry, health matters, and, especially, basic genetics. You will not find all these topics discussed in sufficient depth in ferret books. You must seek out works devoted to them as subjects in themselves, or in large books devoted to other more established pets.

You need to contact people within the hobby who are already in your field of interest, if it involves exhibition. For sales to pet shops, you need to know the trade journals in your country – you will want to advertise in these. You should also discuss the colour pattern and cost needs of pet shops in your area by visiting as many as possible. This gives you some initial contacts for later.

PLANNING FOR BREEDING

Breeding is a serious business and must be treated as such. You would not open a store without a lot of planning, so apply the same criteria to your breeding operation.

HOUSING

You will require a planned breeding room that will probably be an outbuilding. It could be an unused garage, shed, or purpose-built structure. It should have electricity, water, and sewage facilities, otherwise daily chores will be far more difficult. It needs to be well ventilated, dry, and equipped so that its temperature can be regulated at all times. Floors must be easy to clean.

FITTINGS

Fully-equipped cages will be required for each breeding ferret. Although you will start low-key, there must be sufficient space to allow for expansion – more cages, etc. There must be ample easy-clean work surfaces and store cupboards – a refrigerator is almost obligatory in today's high-tech breeding world. Outdoor exercise facilities would be very useful. A ferretry can be designed on the lines of an aviary set-up, each cage or pen having access to its own outdoor run, which need not be large, but will be appreciated by the ferrets.

PERMISSIONS

Before you commence preparations for breeding, you must check whether any local ordinances require a breeding licence and inspection of your facility. Apart from local permissions, you may be subject to regional or national regulation in some countries, which especially include the USA.

RECORDS

You need to keep detailed records of all your breeding endeavours, otherwise you will soon run into problems. Never commit facts and happenings to memory.

BREEDING STOCK

This can either be young and unproven (no previous breeding record), or young proven adults. Owning a male is not a necessity in the initial programme if the services of a good one are available to you. The females may be of a related or unrelated lineage.

They should be from stock registered with an association, and of the highest quality you can afford. Never commence with pet-quality ferrets. When you do obtain a hob, he should be of the highest standard – he will be used on numerous jills. This means that his influence on your stud will be far greater than that of any single female.

By the time you cost the foregoing you will find it adds up to a lot of money, and a lot of time spent preparing the facility in readiness for the stock. Commence low-key, so if things do not work out as hoped, your commitment is minimal to stock. Two jills are ample to start with – you will have lots of ferrets to cope with soon enough.

REALITIES OF BREEDING

Apart from start-up planning and costs, you should fully understand, before you commence, what the practical side entails in terms of time and other factors. There are aspects, and costs, that you may not have thought about, and there are many things that go wrong.

Planning sales: Once you have stock, their needs must be attended to every day – feeding, cleaning and handling them. You must also start thinking about selling your surplus youngsters.

Do not assume buyers are lining up out there; this is wishful thinking – a fault in many beginners. You must plan adverts, and visit pet stores (few offspring will be up to exhibition standard, so pet-quality ones must be sold as well). You must start visiting shows so you become familiar with the way they are run.

Health problems: It is always exciting once the babies are born, but can you cope with the problems? Some may be dead, deformed, or mutilated by the mother, who may abandon one or two, or the whole litter. Everything may go well, but what if babies become ill within days of birth? Can you afford the vet bills, and cope with the trauma? The jill may also become ill, creating a need for hand-rearing or fostering the offspring.

Handling and vaccinations: As the youngsters grow, so will the feed bills. Each baby needs an increasing amount of handling as it nears weaning time. The extent cannot be underestimated if you want buyers to have the same friendly pets that you wanted. Then there are vaccinations and worming costs, as well as possible registration fees.

Stress: Once it is time to sell the babies, you will learn a lot about people. They will telephone you at any time of the day and night. They will want to see the babies, taking up a lot of your time. In

Sexing Ferrets

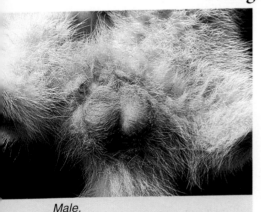

Male.

Female.

The average litter size is between six and nine kits.

many instances, that is the last you will hear from them. You will become frustrated when they want to know why your gorgeous ferrets are more costly than those they have seen elsewhere. They will not add that these were kept in a hutch at the bottom of the garden, were underweight, unvaccinated, and would savagely bite anything that got within teeth range!

Once you sell your babies, a new scenario begins. Some owners will be no problem at all – a joy to sell to. But there are those who telephone in the middle of the night because their pet sneezed! Others who did not even purchase from you will call. They have a problem and were told you were an excellent breeder – the people they purchased from were not interested after the sale was made. These are but a few of the frustrations you will encounter.

Breeding is definitely not for the faint of heart, or those easily upset!

BREEDING FACTS

Sexing: Males are normally larger than females. However, this is an unreliable guide. The best way to sex is to inspect the ano-genital region. The distance between the anus and genitals of the male is longer than in the female. The male's testes are very visible during the breeding period, less so in the winter months.

Breeding age and state: Ferrets become sexually mature at six to eight months old. Breeding from very young individuals is not

At two weeks, the kits will have grown fur, but their eyes and ears do not open until around three weeks.

69

By four weeks, the kits will be increasingly active and alert.

recommended. They should be nine months to a year old and in superb physical condition.

The testes of the male descend into the scrotum during the summer. The vulva of the female starts to swell in the spring and remains in this state until mated. The breeding season is triggered by increasing hours of daylight. The female is an induced ovulator, meaning her eggs are shed by the act of mating, though the male's mere presence may induce this as well.

Mating: It is best to mate a proven hob to an unproven jill, or vice versa. The jill is normally taken to the hob's housing and remains with him until they have mated. If it is clear she is not yet ready to mate she should be removed. Repeat one to two days later. After mating she is returned to her own accommodation. Her vulva will start to recede over the next few weeks, the speed governed by how long she was in heat. She can be palpated for offspring about 30 days after mating. Pseudo-pregnancies are not uncommon in ferrets housed near males, or with other pregnant females.

Gestation period: This is the time between mating and birth of young. In ferrets it is 40-44 days.

Litter size: An average litter will comprise from six to nine kits, but much larger litters are possible.

BREEDING FERRETS

Kit development: Ferrets are born blind, deaf, naked and helpless, but develop rapidly. The ears and eyes open at 22-35 days; the fur is evident at five or more days. The milk or deciduous teeth erupt after about ten days, and the canines appear sometime after 45 days. Kits start to crawl within days of birth, and are being transported back to the nest by the mother when they are ten or so days of age.

Weaning: This is effected by six to nine weeks of age, depending on the size of the litter. Once eating independently, the kits should be removed into nursery housing. They can remain together until they are sold or attain sexual maturity.

Litters per year: In the wild the polecat has one, sometimes two, litters per year, depending on how early in the season the female is mated. Under artificial domestic conditions, a female may have four or more litters; this is not recommended. The drain on the jill's physique would begin to adversely affect the quality and health of her offspring. Two should be regarded as maximum.

Ferrets can be maintained and bred under colony conditions, but this is not advised for the average hobbyist. Non-breeding females can be maintained in their own cage, or in accommodation suitably sized for two or more.

Weaning is well underway at six weeks of age.

8 *Health Care*

Ferrets, like other pets, can fall victim to a legion of problems and diseases. But, if housed and cared for as discussed in this book, you should not experience any more problems than with a dog, cat, or rabbit. Bear in mind your pet can contract illnesses and maladies from other pets in the household, and things like colds from you. Should illness manifest itself, do not try and be a vet, meaning to attempt diagnosis and treatments. This is fraught with dangers.

Many external symptoms of diseases are very similar. Some initially appear like minor problems. How are you to know one from the other? If you make an incorrect diagnosis, or listen to so-called 'expert' friends, the treatment may accelerate the problem. It might also complicate the correct needs once these are known. Play safe and let your vet

do what he or she was trained for, and has the equipment for.

What you can do is know your ferret and its little ways. The more intimate your relationship, the sooner you will know when it is not acting normally, or is displaying problems. The moment you suspect something is wrong, note time, date, and what prompted your concern.

More careful observation is now required so you can spot any other abnormalities. Based on how the problem develops over the next 24 hours, you can decide whether or not to contact your vet, and what immediate action is required.

SIGNS OF ILL HEALTH

The following are signs that something is amiss. They should prompt continued observation, action, or a talk with your vet.

External signs: Weeping eyes, runny nose, swollen nostril(s), misaligned or damaged teeth, bad breath, flaky facial encrustment, wax in ears, any form of swellings or lumps, any abrasions or cuts, loss of hair on any body part, dry lifeless-looking fur, any signs of parasites, blood-streaked faecal matter or urine, evidence of worms around the anus, or in the faecal matter, and diarrhoea.

Behavioural signs: Lethargy, inability to balance correctly, limping, excessive vomiting, coughing, sneezing, excessive scratching, lack of interest in food or water, excessive drinking, syndromes (fur-chewing, pacing, bar-biting, eating faecal matter), excessive sleeping, unwillingness to be handled, pain when handled, excessive panting, wheezy or difficult breathing, straining to pass motions, or any other behaviour that is not normal for your ferret.

When purchasing your pet check to ensure it is displaying none of these signs. Some are indicative of nothing more than minor conditions – but there is no real way of deciding what is minor and what is not. Minor problems rectify themselves within 24 hours. Serious ailments do not. Also, if more than one sign is displayed, this is not good – the more signs, the more dangerous the situation.

RESPONSE TO ILLNESS

Once you suspect something is wrong with your ferret, you must always make some response.

Never do nothing. This gives the problem time to advance. Just by observing more closely, you are at least reacting. If the signs do not prompt great concern, you should review the pet's environment. Has the temperature or the pet's diet changed suddenly? Has the pet been in contact with other non-household pets recently, or are other pets in the family ill? What is the state of the ferret's faecal matter? Could it have eaten some 'off' food, or swallowed bits of a toy – inspect the toys.

At this juncture you must be a sleuth and start making notes, just in case things get worse. An increase of a few degrees in the general environmental temperature is often very successful in treating minor chills. If the pet seems lethargic, and panting, the problem may be that the temperature is too high, so check this. A thermometer located near the housing at all times is useful. It gives the local temperature (that of the cage) as opposed to the general temperature, which is that of the room the cage is in – they may differ a lot in some instances. Once the temperature exceeds 85 degrees F your pet may start to suffer from heat stress.

If the signs are more serious, isolate the ferret from any other pets in the household, and especially from other ferrets. Then discuss the situation with your vet. Faecal samples should be gathered and placed into a phial or similar container – the fingers of disposable surgical gloves are useful for this.

COMMON AILMENTS

While you are not advised to treat internal complaints or diseases, the following ailments will require your immediate attention, pending veterinary advice or treatment, if appropriate.

EXTERNAL PARASITES

These include fleas, lice and ticks. Regular inspection of the coat against its lie reveals these unwanted guests. The use of remedies produced for cats or ferrets will normally be effective. Most treatments are topical (on the skin), but injections of drugs such as Ivermectin can be given subcutaneously by your vet. It is essential, when treating for parasites, that the pet's housing is also treated, as well as the general environment it lives in. If another household pet has parasites, your ferret should be treated as well.

INTERNAL PARASITES

The most common of these are worms and flukes of various species. Normally, the presence of worms goes undetected, but heavy infestations will become apparent and can cause problems, even death. Do not treat for worms unless the species has been identified. This can only be done by faecal examination and egg counts by your vet, who will supply the appropriate treatment.

WOUNDS

These must be cleansed with tepid water to ascertain the extent of

damage. Apply an antiseptic lotion. Minor cuts will heal themselves, but always keep an eye on them in case of secondary infection. More serious wounds require veterinary attention. Wrap the wound with a firm, but not overtight, bandage to stem the blood flow. Transport the pet to the surgery as soon as possible. It may help with bad wounds to wrap the pet in a towel in order to restrict its movements. This will keep it warm and reduce the effects of shock.

HEATSTROKE

The signs are heavy panting, mucous discharge from mouth/nose, vomiting, swollen lips, staring eyes, and collapse. The essential need is to rapidly reduce the ferret's body temperature, especially the head, otherwise permanent brain damage may ensue. First, place the pet in a shaded cool location. Next, dip the body in a bowl of cold water, keeping the head above water. Use a wet cloth to stroke the head. The source of the water is not important, so a hosepipe is an alternative.

As soon as the pet appears to be reviving, offer it a drink. It must be taken to the vet for examination, possible injection to replace vital water fluid loss, and treatment for shock. Heatstroke should not be a problem with a well-cared-for pet; it indicates lack of forethought on the owner's part towards situations that could create the problem.

DIARRHOEA

This is a sign of many problems – too many to list. It is manifested as faecal liquid, foul-smelling and persistent. Mild forms may be caused by a sudden change in the diet, eating excessive amounts of bones, and colds. These cases usually clear up within 24-48 hours. You can help the situation by reducing, or withholding, high-protein foods, especially those high in moisture. Should the condition not clear up, and if other signs become apparent, contact your vet immediately. Chronic diarrhoea can be life-threatening; it will create dehydration and loss of vital water electrolytes that must be replaced rapidly.

HAIRBALLS

Ferrets are fastidious groomers. In the process, especially in their thicker winter coat, they may swallow enough hairs to cause a

partial, or total, blockage of the digestive tract. Initially, they may seem normal, but soon lose interest in their food and start to vomit. You can prevent or treat hairballs by supplying a cat laxative every few weeks, or even a drop of pineapple juice, which breaks the hairballs down. In severe cases, veterinary attention is required.

BURNS AND SCALDS

A burn is usually instantly noticed because the fur is singed or burnt away. Scalds are caused by chemicals or hot liquids and may go unnoticed for longer periods. Both are painful, and thus difficult to treat. Both will sterilise the skin, so the first need is to clear the surrounding area of any dirt, using soap and water. Next, with a burn, any loose or burnt skin should be gently wiped away with a very mild saline solution, before applying a sterile dressing and bandage.

Scalds will leave the hairs intact and these must be carefully clipped away, if possible, before dressing the area as with burns.

Chemical scalds will need to be neutralised if the chemical is known. Use vinegar and water on alkaline burns, bicarbonate of soda on acidic burns. Unless very minor, all burns and scalds should be inspected by your vet at the earliest opportunity.

FIRST-AID KIT

It is always prudent to be ready for problems before they arrive, especially for accidents. If a first aid kit is on hand, this saves valuable time, rather than searching for items when time may be crucial. You can purchase various-sized kits from your vet or pet shop, or you can make up your own, keeping it safe from children and pets.

You might divide it between first aid items for emergencies, and those of a common medicinal nature.

Emergency items: Scissors, straight and curved blunt-ended; tweezers, pointed and blunt-ended; good magnifying glass; fine-toothed comb; rectal thermometer; eye dropper; tongue depressors (also useful as splints); nail-trimmer; 1 cc syringe; pen-light; cotton buds; cotton wool; self-adhesive elastic bandages of various widths; petroleum jelly; gauze pads; eye ointment/liquid; surgical spirits; hydrogen peroxide; antiseptic cream/powder/liquid; styptic powder/crystals/pencil/liquid;

antibacterial ointment; bicarbonate of soda; vinegar; ice packs; towels (paper and cloth).

Medications: Antibiotics (consult with your vet); liquid paraffin or similar laxative; Imodium, Pepto Bismol or similar for stomach upsets; an appropriate pet medicine for colds from your vet; any vet-recommended electrolyte in case of dehydration (to replace vital fluids and minerals); Karo syrup or honey for a quick energy boost; and pure bottled water. Be sure all medicines are stored in cool, dry cupboards or refrigerators. Antibiotics have a finite shelf life: be aware of this if and when obtaining them. Never use antibiotics as preventatives. Overuse or misuse has resulted in many drugs becoming ineffective.

Remember; the best way to avoid problems is to concentrate on sound husbandry practices. Know your ferret, and always be observant for the first signs of abnormality. Totally review your husbandry periodically, and most certainly after any major illness or disease.

BIOLOGICAL DATA

Adult weight: Between 400g and 2kg (14oz and 4lb).
Average size (adult): Between 35 and 62cm (14 and 24in).
Lifespan: Between 6-12 years (in captivity).
Sexual maturity: Between six and eight months.
Breeding season: March to September.
Oestrous cycle: Induced ovulator (eggs are shed by the act of mating).
Gestation: Between 40-44 days.
Litter size: Between six to nine kits.
Development: The kits are born blind, deaf, and naked. Fur is evident within 5-7 days. Eyes and ears open at 22-35 days.
Weaning: Takes place from six to nine weeks.